STOKESAY CASTLE

SHROPSHIRE

Julian Munby FSA and Henry Summerson

Stokesay Castle is a remarkable survival, a fortified manor house that has hardly altered since the late thirteenth century. The house was built by Lawrence of Ludlow, the leading wool merchant of his day, who created a comfortable residence combining an aesthetically pleasing design with some defensive capabilities. In doing so, he took advantage of the newly established peace on the Welsh border, following Edward I's defeat of the rebellious Welsh prince, Llewelyn. This enabled him to build a large hall and a bright, comfortable solar, or private apartment, with windows on to the outside world, without fear of attack.

By good fortune Stokesay escaped relatively unscathed during the Civil War, despite being involved in a minor skirmish. In the nineteenth century the castle was sympathetically repaired and preserved, thanks to the enlightened efforts of several early conservationists. In the 1980s English Heritage carried out an extensive programme of repair.

The Victorian architectural writers Turner and Parker called Stokesay 'altogether … one of the most perfect and interesting thirteenth century buildings which we possess', a description which remains equally true today. This guidebook contains a 'brief tour' of the castle and a plan (inside back cover), a more detailed tour, and a history explaining who lived at Stokesay.

A medieval tile

❖ CONTENTS ❖

*Photographs by the English Heritage Photographic Unit
and copyright of English Heritage, unless otherwise stated*

*Published by English Heritage
23 Savile Row, London W1S 2ET
Visit our website at* www.english-heritage.org.uk
*Copyright © English Heritage 2002
First published by English Heritage 2002
Reprinted 2004, 2005
Edited by Elizabeth Rowe
Designed by Joanna Griffiths
Printed by Matthews
C70, 07/05, Product code 00055, ISBN 1 85074 816 0*

A BRIEF TOUR OF STOKESAY CASTLE

❖

The tour follows the sequence indicated by the numbers.

1) COURTYARD In the Middle Ages several buildings, housing the kitchen and other domestic offices, stood in the courtyard (page 5)

2) HALL The most important room in the castle, the hall was used for meals, entertainment and probably manorial courts (page 8)

3) NORTH TOWER Dating from the thirteenth century, the tower housed comfortable living accommodation (page 13)

4) SOLAR BLOCK The first-floor 'solar' was the private apartment of the lord and his family, and was panelled in oak in the seventeenth century (page 15)

5) PASSAGE BLOCK This building stands against the curtain wall and adjoins the solar block. The second floor was added in the seventeenth century (page 18)

6) SOUTH TOWER Three-storied tower topped by battlements, for which a 'licence to crenellate' was obtained in 1291 (page 19)

7) GATEHOUSE The seventeenth-century timber-framed gatehouse replaced an earlier gatehouse, probably of stone (page 20)

8) CURTAIN WALL Enclosing the castle, these protective stone walls were once much higher, but were 'slighted' during the Civil War (page 30)

Illustration by Terry Ball

INTRODUCTION

Stokesay Castle lies near the centre of the English border with Wales. It shelters in the narrow valley of the River Onny where the road from Ludlow to Shrewsbury breaks through the natural scarp of the Wenlock Edge. This strategic location was recognised long before the castle was built: there are the remains of an Iron Age fort at Norton Camp on the hilltop to the east. Despite its name, Stokesay was not called a castle before the sixteenth century and is really a fortified manor house, more domestic in character than military. As with many early manor houses, the church and castle are now isolated. The late nineteenth-century manor house Stokesay Court lies some two miles away at the southern end of the parish, and the small railway town of Craven Arms is half a mile to the north.

The castle seen from the south-west across the pond

TOUR OF THE CASTLE

❖

This descriptive tour begins inside the castle walls in the courtyard. It leads you through the interior of the main building range on the western side of the courtyard, and finally takes a brief look at the outside. Before reading it, you can familiarise yourself with the castle layout by looking at the brief tour (pages 2–3).

Begin the tour by going through the gateway and into the courtyard.

THE COURTYARD

Around the courtyard are the remains of the curtain walls, now reduced in height or demolished. When the walls were standing at full height the courtyard would have seemed much more enclosed. Beyond these, the castle was surrounded by a water-filled moat, fed by a nearby pond. The entrance would have been guarded by a stone gatehouse, but this was replaced in the seventeenth century by the ornate timber-framed gatehouse you see today.

In the medieval period several buildings, including the kitchen and stables, would have stood around the edges of the courtyard. Later views of the castle show large timber-framed buildings of post-medieval type at each end of the hall. These had domestic functions, again including a kitchen. In the middle of the courtyard stood an oak frame,

The courtyard in 1794, with the timber-framed kitchen

ACTON ARCHIVES

The timber roof covering the well

apparently medieval, supporting a roof over the well. These were all, except the well, removed early in the nineteenth century.

Opposite the entrance is a single range of buildings filling the western side of the courtyard. These form the manor house built by Lawrence of Ludlow in the late thirteenth century, still almost complete and little altered since it was first built.

THE WEST RANGE EXTERIOR

Before entering the building, it is worth looking at some of the details of the exterior. The walls are all built of local stone. The main body of the walls is of mudstone rubble laid in horizontal courses, while the details around the windows and doors are composed of cut blocks of sandstone or mudstone. The roofs are of sandstone slate from Wenlock Edge. The external walls have traces of lime render in many places, and the whole building may have been whitewashed when it was first built.

At the right-hand end of the main range is the north tower. It is of irregular shape, slightly skewed to the alignment of the hall, and with a small turret at the north end. The tower wall that faces the courtyard is of blank masonry (partly rebuilt in the nineteenth century). Against this wall stood the seventeenth-century, timber-framed kitchen, probably replacing an earlier one. On the roof, at the junction with the hall, are twin octagonal chimneys dating from the late thirteenth century.

The west range across the courtyard

In the centre of the range is the hall. Three large windows, each with their own gables, rise above the eaves of the roof. The three buttresses were probably added in the late medieval period to support the walls where the roof trusses had failed; at the same time a half-length window over the door was blocked.

At the south end of the hall is the chamber or solar block. The external staircase was originally of timber and was covered with a lean-to roof, the line of which can still be seen rising up the wall and covering the corner of the half-length window. In the seventeenth century the solar block became the central part of a more comfortable house and a timber-framed extension was built against it, providing additional rooms. The extension was removed in the nineteenth century but its roof-line can be seen below the eaves. It covered the two medieval windows, one of which was replaced by an ogee-headed window to one side of the new building. (The extension can be seen in the illustration on page 5.)

Behind and adjoining the solar block is a building against the curtain wall, known as the passage block (though it leads nowhere).

At the left-hand end is the south tower. This is one of the most interesting parts of the castle, and is planned on a sophisticated

The north tower

The south tower

geometrical base. Two part-dodecagons (12-sided figures) project beyond the angled curtain wall, while the section of the tower inside the courtyard is a part-octagon. The parapet on top is crenellated or battlemented, and has arrow-loops between the openings. Apart from these signs of fortification, however, the pointed lancet windows further down give the tower a domestic rather than a military character. On the east side of the roof a pair of circular chimneys rises above the battlements. Two large medieval buttresses have been added to prevent subsidence on the courtyard side.

Cross the courtyard and enter the hall through the doorway on the right.

Interior of the hall, showing the timber staircase and the cruck roof

THE HALL

This was the principal public room of the manor house, as its impressive size suggests (it measures 31ft x 54ft 6in or 9.5m x 16.6m). The impression of space is increased by the high roof. The walls would originally have been plastered, whitewashed and partially decorated: traces of painted decoration have been found at the northern end. The six large windows (and two half-length ones at the north end) were glazed in the upper half but only shuttered in the lower half; the shutters would therefore have been kept closed in cold or windy weather, making candles or torches necessary within the hall. The south-west window was converted into a door in the eighteenth or nineteenth century, when the hall was used by a local farmer for making cider. The wide pointed doorway into the hall is original, but the nail-studded door dates from the seventeenth century.

The hall would originally have been used for communal meals in which the whole household participated, including the lord and his family, his guests and servants. There would have been long tables down each side, and a larger table across the southern or 'upper' end. This high table may have been on a raised dais, symbolising the status of the most important members of the

BRITISH LIBRARY ADD. 42130

household. An octagonal stone hearth in the floor towards the south end of the hall marks the site of the open fire. Here it would have given most warmth to those sitting at the high table. There must have been an opening to allow the smoke out of the roof, although there is now little evidence of one. A chimney-effect may have been created by blocking in the upper half of the roof trusses on either side of the hearth to capture the rising smoke. There are still fragments of clay infilling in the southern roof truss.

The northern or 'lower' end of the hall was nearest to the service areas, such as the kitchen and buttery. It may have been screened off from the rest of the hall as an area for food preparation, although no trace of a screen survives.

A medieval illustration of a lord dining with his family

The hearth

The household servants may have slept in the hall. Only the lord and his family enjoyed the privilege of private apartments in the solar block which was conveniently situated at the southern end of the hall, near the high table.

Halls of this size and period were normally aisled, with rows of aisle-posts supporting the roof, but by the late thirteenth century there was a growing desire to clear the floorspace under a single roofspan. This was a period of much innovation in roof carpentry, the aim being to do away with the posts and create single-span roofs, often with large timber arches across the hall. Stokesay has a very early example of a cruck roof, in which three pairs of crucks (huge curved timbers) rise from halfway up the wall to the top of the roof, thus clearing the wide span with one truss. Towards the bottom of each cruck, directly below the collar beam, are two curved braces, forming a series of broad rounded arches across the hall. The feet of the crucks rested on stone corbels with geometrical mouldings, but the lower parts rotted and were replaced with stone pilasters (flat pillars against the wall) in the nineteenth century. Most of the outer covering of the roof was also renewed in the 1900s, and the replacement timbers can easily be identified.

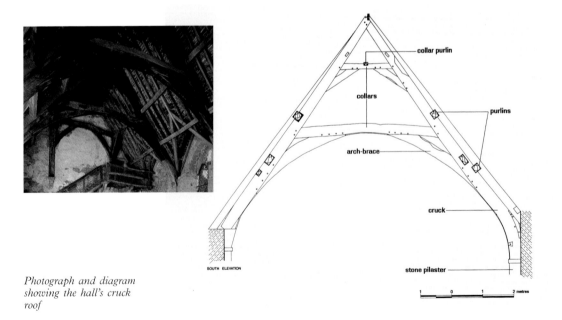

Photograph and diagram showing the hall's cruck roof

THE MEDIEVAL MANOR
❖ OF STOKESAY ❖

Throughout the Middle Ages, Stokesay was the centre of a working estate. In the fourteenth century, there is evidence that the castle was surrounded by fields growing crops, meadows for hay, woods where pigs could forage, a dovecote and gardens producing fruit and vegetables. On one occasion a tenant was fined because his pigs had strayed into the lord's peas.

Stokesay and its estate constituted a manor, that is, a unit whose lord exercised authority over his tenants. Although he could not handle serious offences, the lord could hear 'pleas of debt and trespass' and it was also in his court that he disciplined villagers who failed to care for their houses properly and reminded them that they were required to bring their corn to his mill to be ground into flour.

Around 1400, some of the villagers were still serfs, nominally bound to the soil, and yet it was only in the spring, when they did the ploughing, that these men performed traditional labour services for their lord. At all other times of the year, especially at harvest, the lord hired labourers to work his estates and the serfs paid him cash instead of working themselves. Those estates – his 'demesnes' – provided grain and pastured his cattle. The produce was largely consumed by his household.

However, not everything needed was homegrown. The accounts record purchases of commodities like salt, mustard, cheese, wine and candles, and also of clothes, such as leggings and shoes. In 1423 money was spent on a new granary. There were occasional luxuries. The account for 1425 records that, when the lady of Stokesay had a baby, her husband paid 3s.4d. to three minstrels to celebrate the child's arrival with music.

A medieval farming scene

BRITISH LIBRARY ADD. 42130

The medieval timber staircase

Carpenters' marks (below) and a pair of fourteenth-century sawyers (right)

At the north end of the hall is a timber staircase, one of the most remarkable survivals at Stokesay, since medieval staircases have usually been replaced in later times. It is made with solid timber treads cut from whole tree trunks, and has a moulded handrail with a slot on its underside for a panelled infill. The staircase and gallery are supported on large timber brackets rising from stone corbels on the wall; these closely resemble the hammer-beams that were a new feature of roof construction in the years around 1300.

Both the cruck roof and the timber staircase indicate that the most innovative methods were being used in the building of Stokesay, and that Lawrence of Ludlow was employing a skilled carpenter who was at the forefront in this great period of new and experimental techniques in carpentry. We know that the carpentry is all of one period because a consistent set of carpenters' marks has been used throughout the building. These consist of arcs and circles, rather than the more usual system of numbers, and they occur in pairs on adjacent timbers. They would have been marked on the disassembled pieces of timber, to be matched up on site and raised into position. The marks can be seen on timbers in the hall roof, the north tower and the solar. They were cut using a scribe (a sharp tool), and compass points can be seen in the centres of the circles.

Leave the hall through the low door to the right of the staircase at the north end and go down the steps.

THE NORTH TOWER

The north tower was initially built more for defence than comfort, since its outer walls contain only narrow pointed arrow-loops, but it soon acquired a more domestic character with heated rooms.

The door from the hall is medieval, and made with V-edged planks slotted into each other. The ground floor is a single room lit with narrow window loops. It must have been a service room, probably the buttery, where drink was kept within easy reach of the hall and kitchen. However, traces of red painted scrollwork on the upper parts of the walls, stylistically dated to the early fourteenth century if not earlier, suggest that this room may have been lived in, or perhaps used as a dining room, at one time. In the 1900s traces of a painted portcullis and rose patterns were also visible. The two large ceiling beams braced to posts carry the first-floor joists, simply lodged on top of them as is typical of early flooring. Opposite the door is a small area separated off by a timber frame of uncertain age; this occupies the turret attached to the north end of the tower. It contains a well-shaft connected to the moat, and may have been a scullery.

To reach the first floor, return to the hall and go up the first flight of the timber staircase and through a low doorway.

This floor, now divided in two, was originally a single room lit by narrow window-loops; in the late thirteenth century a wider window, with a trefoiled head, was made in the west wall. This was perhaps a private room, as it seems to have had a fireplace. It may have been divided in two in the mid-seventeenth century, when the fireplace in the south wall was remodelled and the large window opposite was inserted. The southern room has a flagstone floor, while the floor of the northern room is of medieval clay tiles, many of which show traces of decoration. These may have been moved from elsewhere to their present position. They probably date from the end of the thirteenth century.

Red painted scrollwork in the ground-floor room of the north tower

Decorated floor tiles in the north tower

Perhaps at the same time that the rooms were divided, a small latrine was built in the turret, replacing one of the window-loops and separated from the main body of the tower by a lath-and-plaster partition. In the ceiling of the turret the timber joists of the overhanging jetty of the second floor are visible.

Continue up the timber staircase, along the short gallery and through the door on your left into the second-floor apartment.

Reconstructed in the late thirteenth century, this must have been an important private room, with extensive views. The north tower would thus have provided a second suite of rooms at the opposite end of the hall to the main solar block. It may have been intended for the use of guests, or for part of the extended family of the owner. The late thirteenth-century fireplace in the south wall is a fine example of a decorated stone fireplace, with shafts and capitals supporting corbels

The north tower's spacious second-floor apartment

carrying the moulded timber lintel. Above this must have been a timber-and-plaster smoke hood, now only marked by the recess in the wall. To the right of the fireplace is an arched recess, possibly for a lamp.

The north and west walls are timber-framed and project out over the stone walls below. This projection provides a more regular base for the roof and gives a larger floor area inside. The principal wall timbers are medieval, and some bear carpenters' marks like those in the hall roof. Originally the walls were partly filled with clay blockwork, rather than wattle and daub, as was more usual.

We do not know the original window arrangement. The present windows were added in the seventeenth century, and have rounded ovolo mouldings typical of the period. At the same time a plaster ceiling was inserted, parts of which can be seen in the corners of the turret; the door is also seventeenth century. The roof was reconstructed in the nineteenth century, retaining the shape of the thirteenth-century one, which would have been open to view.

Go back down the staircase and across the hall to the small, stone doorway at the south end. This leads into the solar block.

THE SOLAR BLOCK

The solar block is a self-contained, three-storied unit of accommodation adjoined by the passage block, which stands against the curtain wall.

Walk down the modern timber staircase into the basement.

Lit by two windows overlooking the moat, this room was originally a cellar. The great thickness of the walls on three sides suggests that this may be part of a building that predates the main thirteenth-century construction phase. Its medieval use would have been as a storeroom.

When the house was reorganised in the seventeenth century the cellar seems to have become the buttery: the circular marks of barrel-ends can still be seen on the walls. The stones in the floor seem to mark a former partition. The block of masonry in the corner was added in the seventeenth century to buttress the walls above, and a window to light the stairway was inserted at about the same time.

Retrace your steps to the ground floor.

Originally a single room, this space was perhaps a lodging for a household official. It has two windows in the west wall, and there are circular carpenters' marks in the

Detail of a medieval timber door

*One of the cupboards in
the ground-floor solar*

timber doorway, perhaps not in its
original position. The wall next to
the hall contains seventeenth-century
panelling with cupboards.

In the southern room, a doorway
in the south wall leads out to the
passage block. This doorway has
roll-moulded jambs on the outside
and a draw-bar slot on the inside, a
security measure which indicates that
it was once an outside door.

beams indicating that they date from
the same period as the hall roof. The
room was divided in two by a
partition in the seventeenth century
or later, and the partition contains a
hatch, suggesting that this room may
have become a pantry. The northern
room is entered through a medieval

*The living room or 'solar'
with its seventeenth-century
panelling*

*To reach the first floor, return to the
courtyard, climb the staircase to your
right, and at the top go through the
doorway immediately to your right.*

This room is the 'solar', the name
given to the principal first-floor
living room in a medieval house.

It would have been an elegant and comfortable apartment where the lord could entertain in private (as he increasingly did), work and sleep. As was often the case in medieval manor houses, there was no direct access to this room from the hall for security reasons. Instead the room is reached by an external stairway, which was originally covered with a roof to protect the lord and his family from wind and rain as they descended to the hall.

Although many changes were made to the solar in the seventeenth century, it is possible to gain some idea of its thirteenth-century appearance. The windows were much the same as today: at the west end of the room is the original half-length window with window seats, flanked by two lancet windows, while at the east end there was a similar window with one lancet (the present window is a replacement). These large windows, overlooking both the courtyard and the moat, were innovative features at the period, and were a direct result of the period of peace on the Welsh border following the defeat of Llewelyn in 1282. In earlier decades such openness would have been considered too risky, inviting attack.

Another thirteenth-century feature of the solar is the pair of small windows on either side of the fireplace. These overlook the hall

One of the windows looking out from the solar into the hall

and would have allowed the lord to observe activities there without being seen himself. The original fireplace must have been like the one in the north tower, and traces of the original tapering flue can be seen inside the chimney. The solar was originally open to the roof (the roof timbers still survive above the seventeenth-century ceiling).

Evidence of a later decorative feature, but still predating the seventeenth-century changes, was found when the panelling around the room was removed for cleaning: in the recess of the west window Tudor roses are painted on to the plaster (they have now been re-covered).

In the seventeenth century the solar was completely refitted, probably by the Baldwyn family,

A Tudor rose revealed in the window recess during cleaning

who seem to have used it as a dining room. The walls and window recesses were covered in oak panelling and a ceiling was installed. A new extension was added against the eastern wall of the building, the original east window was filled in and a new window made in the corner. Another new window was added in the south wall. The east window was reopened when the panelling was removed from it in the early nineteenth century.

The woodwork in the solar is Jacobean in style. It is comparable with early seventeenth-century work elsewhere in the county: for example, there is a similar overmantel at Brogyntyn in the north-west of the county, dated 1617. At Stokesay, however, the overmantel is believed to have been installed in the middle of the century, so perhaps it was made at an earlier date and brought here from elsewhere. The panelling is in sections between decorated columns, and above it are a frieze and cornice. The woodwork was originally painted: traces of at least two early colour schemes have been found on the panelling and overmantel, with a wide range of colours including varieties of gold, pink, red, green and white. The fireplace was remodelled with a plain segmental arch and brick back. The richly carved overmantel has five columns containing half-figures, interspersed with four panels, the two in the centre containing monstrous heads in strapwork surrounds. The overmantel is of Flemish origin (or inspiration), and is probably based on the busy 'grotesque' designs featured in contemporary pattern-books and engravings.

The stone doorway in the south-west corner of the room originally led on to a wall-walk above the single-storey room below; it has a hole for a draw-bar, showing it was once an external door. In the seventeenth century the curtain wall was increased in height and given a pitched roof; this resulted in the creation of a new room, reached by a short passageway with a small window. In the new room a window and a latrine were built in the place

A central panel in the elaborate overmantel

of battlements on the west side, while another window looks on to the courtyard. The latrine replaces an earlier one on the wall-walk and emptied into the moat; it has a seventeenth-century door and shows traces of red and black wall-painting.

Leave the solar and walk over the timber drawbridge leading from the external staircase into the south tower.

THE SOUTH TOWER

The south tower provided a series of self-contained apartments, given status by their comparative remoteness of access, and yet connected to the hall and the solar block. The exact function of the tower is uncertain, but there are several possibilities. It may have served as sleeping quarters for the lord and his family, with the solar being used for eating and private entertainment. Alternatively, the tower could have provided a spacious suite of rooms for guests, or, like the north tower, it might have accommodated different generations of an extended family.

The sawn-off ends of the lifting gear for the drawbridge, now covered with lead, can be seen above the door into the tower. The first floor consists of one large room, containing a fireplace, latrine, four

windows with window seats, and wall recesses. Although the windows are narrow, their wide splays increase the amount of light entering the room, so that this must have been a bright, comfortable apartment. As in the solar, the fireplace was renewed in the seventeenth century, while the ceiling beams are probably sixteenth century. In the entrance lobby a pointed doorway gives access to the wall stairs leading up to the roof.

Windows in the south tower's first-floor apartment

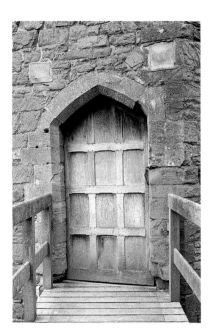

The door leading into the south tower

You can reach the second floor via the staircase from the first floor.

At the stairhead is a latrine, in a short passage outside the room. On this level there are five windows with window seats (one double), a fireplace and a wall recess, making a spacious and well-lit apartment similar to the one below. In the north wall, by the stairs to the roof, is a blocked door now containing two small windows. A door at this height can hardly have been reached from an external staircase, and its purpose may have been to allow the lifting of furniture such as beds and chests that were too large to be brought up the narrow staircase. The roof has some moulded sixteenth-century beams and is otherwise modern, but the stone corbels indicate the base of the original roof.

Take the wall staircase up again to the battlements.

A further staircase leads up to a small turret. The top of the tower gives extensive views over the surrounding country, and shows its commanding position at the head of the valley. The parapet top is chamfered, and the square openings (embrasures) have external rebates and hooks for shutters, to protect those standing on the battlements. The walls between the openings (merlons) contain splayed cross-shaped arrow-loops for crossbows.

Return down the staircases and out into the courtyard. The ground floor of the tower can be entered through the pointed doorway.

The ground-floor interior is spacious, with four windows on the south side, and wall recesses that may have held lights. The fireplace in the east wall was added when the house was deserted and a smithy was established here; this caused a fire in the early nineteenth century that completely gutted the tower.

THE GATEHOUSE

Of the post-medieval additions to the castle, only the gatehouse now remains; it is similar to the Council House Gatehouse in Shrewsbury, dated 1620, and is likely to have been built about 20 years later. The highly decorated exterior is an elaborate example of the regional style of timber framing, built around a central gate passage and overhanging (jettied) on all sides at the first floor. There is an original brick chimney-stack in the northern half of the building, and a modern one at the south end. Each storey is differently decorated, the ground floor with close studding and the

Carvings of Adam and Eve on the gatehouse

The timber-framed gatehouse (left) is similar to the Council House Gatehouse in Shrewsbury (below)

first floor with square panels in lozenge patterns (and arched panels below the windows), while the four gables have quarter-circle braces.

The gate, which is cross-planked and nail-studded, is on the courtyard side; within it is a small wicket gate. The gateposts have fluted columns and bases supporting carved heads and there are also elaborate carved heads on the corner-posts. Flanking the central first-floor windows are posts carved as pilasters while the overhanging first-floor jetties are moulded and the gable barge-boards intricately carved. Outside the castle, the carvings around the outer entrance represent the Garden of Eden, with Adam and Eve on either side of the Tree of Knowledge. Other carvings include grotesque figures, fierce dragons and foliage designs that may contain emblematic references, a common feature of this period.

EXTERIOR OF THE CASTLE

A walk along the moat around the outside of the castle gives an impression of how it would have appeared to an approaching traveller, a combination of impressive fortification and comfortable residence. Certain features of the design clearly indicate that Lawrence was as concerned to impress with the elegance of his house as with its strength.

The moat is entirely artificial, as the castle stands on a slope. The water came from a large pond to the south-west of the castle, which had a retaining dam and may have been used as a fish-pond. There may have been a wider landscaped setting at one time.

The west range exterior

The north tower stands on a sloping (battered) base that is lower than the rest of the castle. The brick drain of the seventeenth-century latrine can be seen on the west wall of the turret. The construction of the timber jetty of the top floor is visible, together with the series of stone corbels supporting the brackets.

From the west, the main range of buildings appears to advantage, and this may have been intended as the main façade of the castle, since the road from Ludlow may originally have passed on this side of the valley. Lawrence's desire to create an aesthetically pleasing impression can be seen in the attempted symmetry of the elevation, with the hipped roof of the north tower matching that of the solar block, and the three full-length windows of the hall flanked by half-windows at each end.

The geometric plan of the south tower can best be appreciated from the outside. The windows, whose arrangements seemed bewildering from inside the tower, can now be seen to be disposed in regular formation. The effect is imposing and castle-like, but hardly serious defensive architecture; instead this seems to have been a 'display' front for long-distance views of the castle. From this vantage point the tower would have resembled a double-towered castle gatehouse until seen at close range.

View across the courtyard towards the church

To the north of the castle is the Church of St John the Baptist, its churchyard extending almost to the castle walls. The churchyard formerly contained a fine stone dovecote, probably of medieval date. The church is built on a small, two-cell plan of nave and chancel, with a west tower. The south door is Norman but the rest of the church was much rebuilt in 1654-64 following damage in the Civil War, and is an unusual example of a church built at this period. Inside there is some fine seventeenth-century woodwork, and the walls bear large inscriptions of the Ten Commandments and other texts.

HISTORY
OF THE CASTLE

❖

Stokesay's history is closely connected with its position near the Welsh border. As far back as the eighth century Welsh raids were troubling the Mercian King Offa and border disputes, attacks and forays continued to present problems for William the Conqueror and his barons. The threat became more urgent when the Princes of Gwynedd, Llewelyn the Great and later his grandson, Llewelyn ap Gruffydd, united the various princedoms of Wales under one banner. Their resistance was determined and powerful but they were eventually forced to submit to English power by Edward I, although it was not until 1284 that Wales was finally brought under English rule. It is no coincidence that Stokesay Castle was built at about this time, for this was the first period of relative peace the area had known for centuries.

FEUDAL ORIGINS

The first records of Stokesay date from the period immediately following the Norman Conquest. William installed Roger Montgomery as Earl of Shrewsbury, and he in turn granted Stokesay to one of his retainers, Roger of Lacy. In Domesday Book (1086), Lacy is shown as the owner of Stokesay (or 'Stoches', as it was then called), while the pre-Conquest owner,

The death of Llewelyn in 1282, as depicted in a medieval manuscript

BRITISH LIBRARY ADD. 42130

Aldred, is recorded as being a landholder in nearby Aldon. The chief Lacy manor was at Stanton Lacy, and later at Ludlow; after Stanton, Stokesay was the most valuable Lacy holding. There is no mention of a castle at Stokesay in Domesday, but the land did include a mill and, unusually, a beekeeper.

Another Marcher lord given land by Roger Montgomery was Picot, also called Robert of Say, who came from Sai in the French département of Orne. The land was around Clun, some nine miles (14km) west of Stokesay (see page 35). By the early twelfth century a descendant of Picot's, Theoderic de Say, had become the Lacys' tenant at 'South Stoke'. It was from the name Say that the manor eventually came to be known as Stokesay.

The Say family were tenants until the death of Walter de Lacy in 1240, when his son-in-law John de Verdon inherited, and obtained possession of South Stoke from Hugh de Say in exchange for lands in Ireland. John was amongst the Marcher lords required by Henry III to live on their estates to counter the threats of Welsh raids. It is possible that he began building at Stokesay. By 1270 John de Verdon had gone on crusade, letting the manor in his absence, and his son continued to live elsewhere and let the estate after his father's death in 1274.

THE MERCHANT'S MANOR HOUSE

Verdon's tenant John de Grey sold the tenancy of Stokesay to the merchant Lawrence of Ludlow in 1281, confirming the sale for the price of a 'juvenile sparrow hawk'. Lawrence's father Nicholas was a considerable wool merchant, selling the fine wools of the Welsh borderlands, which were some of the best in England. Lawrence probably began his career as Nicholas' partner and, after his father's death in around 1279, he continued to export wool to the Low Countries, where the cloth industry had a seemingly insatiable appetite for English wool. His profits were such that he was able to lend money to the king, and

The coats of arms of the Stokesay families

Shearing sheep in the Middle Ages

A reconstruction drawing of Stokesay Castle as it may have appeared at the end of the thirteenth century

TERRY BALL

also to many of the great men of the Welsh marches, such as the Earl of Arundel and the Mortimers of Wigmore and Chirk. The problem for people with money was what to do with it (there were no banks in the Middle Ages) and the obvious answer was to invest in landed property. Lawrence is one of the earliest recorded English examples of a man who became rich in trade setting himself up as a country gentleman and thus acquiring status,

as well as a legacy for his children.

Stokesay was in a convenient location for Lawrence, since it lay on the road from Ludlow, his family's place of origin, to Shrewsbury, the centre of their business. Although he remained technically a feudal tenant of de Grey and Verdon, he was for most purposes the owner of the whole manor, obtaining a royal charter of free warren (hunting rights) in 1281, and extending his manorial grazing rights in 1288.

A generation later, on the death of his son in 1316, the manor comprised nearly 200 acres, including two mills, a dovecote and a wood, and generated a substantial income through rents and other sources.

Lawrence did not stop trading on moving to Stokesay, not least because he needed money for his construction work. The investment in building activity on the scale seen at Stokesay is remarkable, especially since most of the existing structure seems to be of one date. We can assume that Lawrence began building soon after 1281, while the completion of his work is perhaps indicated by the 'licence to crenellate' which he obtained in 1291 from Edward I at Hereford. This was a licence granted by the king allowing the licence-holder to make a structure defendable by adding battlements. The idea was that such a right would be granted only to the king's allies, who would not use their newly acquired defences against the Crown. Some form of defence was considered particularly desirable in vulnerable border areas such as this, and was also a fashionable status symbol. In the words of the grant Lawrence could 'build and crenellate his manor at Stokesay with a wall of stone and lime', and there is little doubt that this permission was applied to the south tower and probably also to the curtain wall and gatehouse. Despite this superficially aggressive exterior reminiscent of castellated architecture, however, Stokesay was always regarded as a manor house and could hardly have resisted a determined attack.

Lawrence was not to enjoy his new home for long. In 1294 a consortium of merchants agreed to raise money from wool exports for Edward I to finance his allies in the war with France. As head of the consortium, Lawrence commanded the wool fleet as it sailed from London for the Low Countries, but his ship was wrecked off Aldeburgh and he was drowned. His body was brought back to Ludlow for burial.

A ship being loaded in a Flemish port

The coats of arms of the Ludlow family members

The monastic chronicler of Dunstable Priory (itself no small wool-trader) gleefully records his death, 'drowned in a ship of wool … because he sinned against the wool mongers'. After Lawrence's death the firm continued, however, and both his wife and brother John were major exporters of wool.

Many generations of Ludlows succeeded Lawrence and evidently became well established as county gentry, frequently serving as Sheriffs of Shropshire in the fourteenth and fifteenth centuries. Anne, the last Ludlow heiress, married Thomas Vernon, who died at Stokesay in 1563. He was succeeded by his

❖ HENRY VERNON ❖

Henry Vernon was a colourful character who was nearly ruined by his unsuccessful attempts to claim the barony of Powys. So determined was he to prove his noble ancestry that he concocted a bizarre story that the last Lord Powys' signature on his deed of conveyance had been forged posthumously by conspirators who opened his coffin, put a pen in the corpse's hand and with it traced his

signature on the document. Henry Vernon haunted the courts for decades with this tale, brushing aside moments of farce as when vital documents were found to have been nibbled into illegibility by mice.

For many years Vernon lived lavishly, on borrowed money according to his enemies. He bought fine clothes: in 1576, for instance, he paid for 'a white canvas doublet wavy laid with

white silk lace' and 'a new taffeta hat with a bugle band and a black sprig in it'. He also bought a brush for his beard and in February 1583 he spent 2d on 'potata roots'. It was not in fact extravagance that effectively ruined him but his standing surety for the debt of another man who defaulted. By the end of 1591 he was in the Fleet Prison. He was released in 1592 but his fortunes never recovered.

grandson Henry Vernon, who was forced to sell his estates to pay his crippling debts. In 1598 Stokesay itself had to go, sold to Sir George Mainwaring, another Shropshire landowner, for £6000. The park first appears on Saxton's map of Shropshire of 1577 and at the time of the sale is recorded as being stocked with red and fallow deer. The Mainwarings sold the manor in 1617 and in 1620 Stokesay manor and castle, together with other Shropshire properties, were bought by Dame Elizabeth Craven and her young son William. The price was £13,500 – several millions in modern money.

THE CRAVENS AND THEIR TENANTS

William Craven seems to have spent little time at Stokesay, preferring fighting to farming, although he did employ a farm manager who reared cattle, sheep and horses at Stokesay. Craven spent a lot of money on the castle in the 1630s before letting it to Charles Baldwyn who intended to 'spend the residue of his days there'. It was probably Charles who built the new gatehouse in about 1640-41, and he may also have added the kitchen and other buildings in the courtyard, now demolished. Charles was MP for Ludlow until 'disabled'

WILLIAM CRAVEN

William Craven (1608–97), son of the Lord Mayor of London, inherited a fortune at the age of ten, and became Lord Craven of Hampsted Marshall in 1627. Though very short, he wanted above all else to be a soldier. There were no opportunities in England in the 1620s, so he went abroad and served in the Dutch army against the Spaniards. He went to Germany in 1632, to fight for the Protestant cause in the Thirty Years War, and again in 1637, where he fought alongside Charles I's nephew Prince Rupert. The two young men were captured together and Craven spent two years as a prisoner.

It was while serving abroad that Craven came to know Prince Rupert's romantic mother, the so-called 'Winter Queen' of Bohemia, and formed what seems to have been a deep but entirely platonic attachment to her. When Elizabeth of Bohemia returned to England in 1661, Craven gave her a home in his own London residence. He was generous in other respects too and in 1665, the year in which he was made Earl of Craven, he donated land for the burial of the victims of the Great Plague of London. His efforts during the Great Fire were notable and it was said that his horse was trained to recognise the smell of smoke so that when a fire broke out he could hasten to the rescue. During the Glorious Revolution Craven demonstrated his loyalty to James II by refusing to discharge his men from Whitehall without a command from the king. Thereafter Craven lived quietly until he died in 1697, aged nearly ninety.

Above: William Lord Craven: a portrait of 1647

NATIONAL PORTRAIT GALLERY

(or stripped of his powers) for supporting Charles I, and was later fined for 'delinquency' (another offence arising from his support for the king) by Parliament.

Charles' son, Sir Samuel Baldwyn, was a lawyer and later also MP for Ludlow. He was probably involved in the short siege of the castle that took place in 1645, during the Civil War. Following the capture of Shrewsbury, 500 foot and 300 horse were dispatched by Parliament to take Ludlow, and on the journey they came to Stokesay. The ensuing events are described in the following contemporary account:

Title page from a contemporary account of the taking of Stokesay Castle in the Civil War

> The place was conceived considerable, therefore the next morning wee drew up to it, and summoned it, but the Governor Captain Dauret refused; thereupon wee prepared for a storme, being ready to fall on, gave a second summons, which was hearkened unto, a parley admitted, and the castle delivered up, and is now garrisoned by us.

So began and ended the one recorded military encounter at Stokesay, though a more serious battle took place shortly afterwards. At the foot of Norton Camp the besieged garrison of Ludlow vainly attempted to attack the Parliamentary army, with the loss of 100 men and 360 prisoners. After the siege the castle was ordered to be 'slighted' (literally 'levelled'), but little more seems to have been done than the demolition of the curtain walls in 1647.

In the following year Samuel Baldwyn married, and his father settled on him 'Stokesay Castle, Togeather with all Barnes, Stables, outhouses and buyldings belonging to the same, and also… Stoke Mills', a park and fishery. Samuel prospered in his legal career, being knighted in 1673, and was buried in the Temple Church in London. His monument describes him as being 'of Stoke Castle', and there is little doubt that Stokesay was his country home. He was assessed for Hearth Tax in 1673/4 on a total of 17 hearths. The panelling of the solar and the new windows in the north tower have been attributed to Samuel, who clearly made the castle a comfortable home; he also devoted his energies to the rebuilding of the church. On Samuel's death in 1683 his son Charles, another lawyer and Recorder of Ludlow, became the last of the Baldwyn family to live at Stokesay and, some time after his death in 1706, the castle ceased to be occupied, though a visitor in about 1730 refers to portraits still hanging in the solar.

REDISCOVERY AND REPAIR

For 150 years the castle was used by farmers as an adjunct to the nearby farm; the buildings gradually grew dilapidated and by the early nineteenth century they were in a very poor state. At about this period, however, interest in Gothic architecture was beginning to develop, and the importance of Stokesay was soon recognised. Britton included it in his *Architectural Antiquities of Great Britain* (1814), and Turner and Parker's *Domestic Architecture in England* (1851) described it as being 'altogether …

This engraving by S and N Buck dates from 1731

THE SOUTH WEST VIEW OF STOKE CASTLE, IN THE COUNTY OF SALOP.

To the Rt. Honble WILLIAM Lord CRAVEN
Baron of Hamsteac: Marshall in the County of Berks
This Prospect is humbly Inscrib'd by:
Yr Lordship's most Obedt Servts
Saml & Nathl Buck.

THIS CASTLE stands upon the River Kern: it antiently belong'd to ye Family of Verdun. Issue male failing in Theobald de Verdun, it went by his Daughter Elizabeth and her Daughter Isabel by Marriage to Henry Lord Ferrers of Groby, who died in 17. Ed. III. It continu'd in this Noble Family for many succes sions; in that branch of it call'd Ferrers of Tamworth, but it is now in ye Noble Family of Craven W. Lord Craven of Hampsted Marshal being the present Lord thereof.

❖ MRS STACKHOUSE ACTON ❖

BY KIND PERMISSION OF EJH LENNOX

Born in 1794, Frances Stackhouse Acton was the eldest daughter of Thomas Andrew Knight of Downton Castle, the co-founder of the Royal Horticultural Society. She had little formal schooling and preferred to help her father with his botanical studies and to enjoy the company of his erudite friends, who included the scientist Sir Humphrey Davy and Sir Joseph Banks, the botanist who had sailed with Captain Cook aboard the *Endeavour*. At the age of 17, she married Thomas Pendarus Stackhouse of Acton Scott Hall. The couple had one daughter, who died in 1830. Five years later, Mrs Stackhouse Acton lost her husband after a long illness.

Still only in her early forties, Mrs Stackhouse Acton devoted herself to local activities. She became a noted antiquarian and artist and published and illustrated several books such as *The Garrisons of Shropshire* and *The Castles and Mansions of Shropshire*. She excavated and catalogued the Roman villa at Acton Scott, built and embellished several cottages on the estate and erected the village school in a neo-Tudor style. Although living in a rather remote part of the country and visiting London infrequently, Mrs Stackhouse Acton numbered amongst her acquaintances two prime ministers – Lord Aberdeen and Lord John Russell – and the eminent geologists Sir Roderick Murchison and Sir Charles Lyell. She died at Acton Scott Hall in 1881, having been a widow for 46 years.

Mrs Stackhouse Acton (left, in a portrait of 1820 by H Edridge) and one of her watercolours (below)

Interior of Court Stoke-Say Castle

ACTON ARCHIVE

one of the most perfect and interesting thirteenth century buildings which we possess'. The record of their visit in 1845 shows that the courtyard buildings had already been removed (in about 1830) and the feet of the crucks in the hall roof had been replaced with stonework.

Moves to preserve the castle buildings were initiated in about 1850 by Mrs Stackhouse Acton (1794–1881) of Acton Scott (a village about six miles or 10km north of Stokesay); she urged Lord Craven to repair the buildings, and contributed to the serious study of the castle in several publications. In 1869 JD Allcroft, an altruistic Victorian, purchased Stokesay and carried out repairs from then until his death in 1893. His aim was to preserve the buildings for the future, and he resisted the temptation, to which many of his contemporaries succumbed, to 'restore' the buildings in a way that would now be considered unsympathetic. His son continued this programme of conservative repair under the auspices of the Society for the Preservation of Ancient Buildings. Without the efforts of the Allcrofts, Stokesay would certainly not be in its present remarkable state of preservation. The Allcroft family opened the castle to the public in 1908 and in 1992, following the death of Lady Magnus Allcroft, the castle came into the guardianship of English Heritage.

Two vintage photographs of the castle

NATIONAL MONUMENTS RECORD

❖ J D ALLCROFT ❖

John Derby Allcroft (1822-93) had a great deal in common with his predecessor at Stokesay, Lawrence of Ludlow. Both men came from the Anglo-Welsh borders and both followed their fathers into the business that made their fortunes. In Allcroft's case, the business was making leather gloves and, above all, ladies' gloves. In the nineteenth century gloves became an essential accessory for every fashion-conscious woman. From 1846 Allcroft was effectively the head of the company. Business flourished under his management and by the mid-1880s the company was selling over a million pairs of gloves every year.

An outstanding example of a mid-Victorian businessman, Allcroft had many of the moral virtues that were then almost

BY KIND PERMISSION OF SIR LAURIE AND LADY MAGNUS

A portrait of JD Allcroft by F Grant, with a painting of Stokesay behind (1873)

automatically associated with material success. He was frugal, industrious and attentive to detail. Every day he walked from his house in Lancaster Gate to his office in Cheapside and back again in the evening. Hard on himself, he demanded very high standards from his workforce, but

was a just and generous employer and greatly respected by his employees. A committed evangelical Christian, he built three London churches and gave money generously to charities like the Royal Hospital for Incurables.

Allcroft effectively retired in 1873 and, again like Lawrence of Ludlow, he set himself up as a country gentleman, having bought the Stokesay estate in 1869. He built himself a splendid mansion called Stokesay Court and set about restoring the castle's medieval buildings with what was then a very unusual concern for preserving the original materials – as *Country Life* put it in 1910, he had left these 'untouched, even in respect of their surfaces'. By the time Allcroft died on 29 July 1893, Stokesay had been comprehensively repaired.

From 1986–89 English Heritage carried out a comprehensive programme of repair at Stokesay. The castle's condition before repair was described as 'not one of abject decay and absolute neglect, but … rather starved and worn out'. The object was, with minimal intervention, to reduce deterioration by skilful mending, while maintaining the 'essential rustic quality of the monument'. It was intended that 'within a short period our activities over three or four years will be scarcely obvious, except perhaps to the most discerning eye'.

CLUN CASTLE

TOUR AND DESCRIPTION

Nearly nine miles (14.5km) to the west of Craven Arms and 16 miles (26km) by road from Ludlow lies Clun, now a quiet, picturesque country town but once a flourishing Norman settlement. On a motte or mound high above the River Clun, which cuts through the town, stand the remains of Clun Castle. What you see today is a section of the curtain wall and two flanking, half-round towers, while the site is dominated by the four-storey Great Tower built into the side of the mound.

Despite extensive documentary evidence, it is now very difficult to visualise the full extent of the castle's buildings. A report from 1272 describes the castle as being small but strongly built with a bailey or court outside, while an inquisition post mortem of 1440 mentions a chapel, a well and a great grange, as well as gardens within the bailey.

Obviously there was once a lively and busy settlement here.

Generally referred to as the Keep, the Great Tower has flat clasping buttresses on the northern corners and, from the outside, the broken window openings appear to have semi-circular or segmental heads. There are four main floors in all, with additional upper floors in the two northern corner watch-towers.

Built of the same local rubblestone as the Great Tower, the two round towers and wall appear to date from slightly earlier. The round plan of the towers suggests a mid-thirteenth-century date while the Great Tower was probably built in about 1300 and deliberately designed to echo the great Norman keeps of the twelfth century.

The Great Tower at Clun

THE NORTH WEST VIEW OF CLUN CASTLE, IN THE COUNTY OF SALOP.

To John Walcot Esq.
Owner of these Remains.
This Prospect is gratefully Inscribed by
Y.'' most Humble Serv.''
Sam.'' & Nath.'' Buck.

A Buck engraving of Clun Castle from 1731

Further Reading

RA Cordingley, 'Stokesay Castle, Shropshire: The Chronology of its Buildings', *Art Bulletin*, Vol. xlv (1963)
JT Smith, 'Stokesay Castle', *Archaeological Journal*, Vol. cxiii (1956)
RJ Tolley, C Babington and G Chitty, 'Stokesay Castle, Shropshire: The Repair of a Major Monument', *Transactions of the Association for Studies in the Conservation of Historic Buildings* (ASCHB), Vol. 15 (1990)
M Wood, 'Thirteenth-Century Domestic Architecture in England', *Art Bulletin*, Vol. cx (1950)

HISTORY

Although the first mention of Clun Castle does not appear until the 1140s, the original motte and bailey construction was perhaps established on the site of the pre-Conquest manor in the late eleventh century. It seems likely that its builder was Picot de Say, the chief vassal of Roger de Montgomery. Picot had received the estates of Clun and Stokesay from Roger, who had in turn been granted them by William the Conqueror.

Shortly before July 1155, William Fitz Alan of Oswestry acceded to the Clun lordship. Under the Fitz Alans, Clun Castle suffered a number of attacks and assaults. In 1196 Rhys, Prince of South Wales, reduced the castle to a pile of ashes and in 1215 John Fitz Alan rebelled against King John, who responded by sending troops. The 1200s and 1300s were Clun's glory days for it was during this period that the castle acted as the Fitz Alans' main residence. Edward I spent the night there on 18 June 1295, a sign of the wealth of the Fitz Alans who drew a great deal of their money from their marcher estates, Clun among them. In 1370 the third earl lent 10,000 marks (£6666.13s.4d.) to the king.

Devastation around Clun by followers of Owain Glyndŵr in the early fifteenth century helped end the prosperity. By 1539 there were reports that the castle was 'somewhat ruinous' and, although the Fitz Alan family and their descendants remained the owners until 1677, they had probably not been living at Clun for some time. A janitor was paid there for the last time in 1589–90. The castle seems to have played no part in the Civil War but its romantic nature was noted by Sir Walter Scott who, legend has it, wrote *Betrothed* while staying at Clun and based the Garde Doloreuse on the castle. In 1894 the then Duke of Norfolk purchased the castle, 'presumably as a symbolic gesture to his family's ancestry', and it has remained the property of the Dukes of Norfolk ever since. It is now in the guardianship of English Heritage.